MYTHOLOGY OF THE WORLD

HEROES AND VILLAINS OF WORLD MYTHOLOGY

by Clara MacCarald

BrightPoint Press

San Diego, CA

© 2023 BrightPoint Press
an imprint of ReferencePoint Press, Inc.
Printed in the United States

For more information, contact:
BrightPoint Press
PO Box 27779
San Diego, CA 92198
www.BrightPointPress.com

ALL RIGHTS RESERVED.

No part of this work covered by the copyright hereon may be reproduced or used in any form or by any means—graphic, electronic, or mechanical, including photocopying, recording, taping, web distribution, or information storage retrieval systems—without the written permission of the publisher.

LIBRARY OF CONGRESS CATALOGING-IN-PUBLICATION DATA

Name: MacCarald, Clara, author.
Title: Heroes and Villains of World Mythology / by Clara MacCarald.
Description: San Diego, CA: BrightPoint Press, 2023 | Series: Mythology of the World | Includes bibliographical references and index. | Audience: Grades 7–9
Identifiers: ISBN 9781678204969 (hardcover) | ISBN 9781678204976 (eBook)
The complete Library of Congress record is available at www.loc.gov.

CONTENTS

AT A GLANCE   4

INTRODUCTION   6
THE SUN SLAYER

CHAPTER ONE   12
ON A QUEST

CHAPTER TWO   24
MONSTER SLAYERS

CHAPTER THREE   36
AT WAR

CHAPTER FOUR   48
MYTHICAL LEADERS

Glossary   58
Source Notes   59
For Further Research   60
Index   62
Image Credits   63
About the Author   64

AT A GLANCE

- Many heroes must go on a quest to accomplish a specific goal. They often face villains at home or along the way.

- The purpose of quests may be to obtain objects. In a Greek myth, the hero Jason went on a quest to find the Golden Fleece. Quests may also involve reaching a certain place.

- Heroes may slay monsters during their quests. Marduk faced the monster Tiamat in Babylonian mythology.

- Sometimes villains force heroes to face monsters. In Norse mythology, the villain Regin challenged the hero Sigurd to slay the dragon Fafnir.

- Heroes may be leaders during wars. The Chinese emperor Huang Di fought Chiyou's army of demons.

- Some heroes fight armies alone, while other heroes lead a group of warriors. Two heroines named Hervor led armies in Norse mythology.

- Villains are sometimes kings. One example is the evil King Lycaon in Greek mythology.

- Heroes who lead their people can do great deeds. The Chinese hero Yu stopped a great flood.

INTRODUCTION

THE SUN SLAYER

The world has only a single sun today. But a Chinese myth says there were once ten suns. They rested on the branches of a great tree. The tree grew in a valley and rose above the mountains. As day approached, one sun would climb to the top of the tree. The other suns waited their turn.

One day the suns grew bored. All of them took to the sky at once. They vowed to never leave. The earth quickly grew

The sun is a common topic in mythology. Many ancient cultures had a god or goddess who they believed controlled the sun.

The hero Yi stopped the suns from destroying the world. He used his bow and arrow to shoot nine of the suns out of the sky.

dangerously hot. Something had to be done. King Yao asked the hero Yi for help.

Yi took up his bow and aimed at the suns. One by one he released his arrows. The suns fell to the ground. In one **version** of the story, Yao told Yi to shoot nine. In another, Yao stole one of Yi's arrows so the hero couldn't knock down all ten. In the end, only a single sun remained to light the world thanks to the actions of a hero.

HEROES AND VILLAINS

Heroes and villains play important parts in mythologies around the world. Heroes can be gods. But they are often human. Even then, heroes are no mere mortals. They have greater strength or abilities than ordinary people. Villains often oppose heroes.

Many heroes are known for their struggles. They may perform hard tasks. They might slay evil monsters or fight difficult battles. Other heroes gain fame by teaching people arts or other skills.

Mythical heroes don't always achieve victory. Their stories may end in sadness thanks to villains or the heroes' own weaknesses. Some heroes find early

Many heroes display great courage fighting other warriors. Sometimes, though, their enemies win the battles.

success only to lose it in the end. But hero myths inspire the listeners to aim for greatness in their own lives.

1
ON A QUEST

Many myths feature a hero working toward a goal. The hero often resists leaving home at first. But heroes are driven to help others. Along the way, heroes encounter villains and other challenges. Whether they achieve their goals or not, heroes have changed in a meaningful way by the time they return home.

QUEST FOR A GOD

In Egyptian mythology, the god Osiris and the goddess Isis ruled over the world. They were heroes to the people. Thanks to the

Osiris remained a powerful god even after his death. The ancient Egyptians believed that Osiris made the Nile River flood each year.

Gods and men weren't the only heroic characters in mythology. Goddesses such as Isis (pictured) and women also went on important quests in some stories.

divine couple's teachings on farming, no one ever went hungry. Life in Egypt felt like paradise.

But Osiris's brother Seth deeply envied Osiris. Seth plotted to kill his brother. He created a beautiful box the exact size and shape of Osiris. He then offered the box to anyone who could fit inside it. When Osiris stepped in, Seth sealed the box and tossed it into the Nile River. Seth became king.

Isis found Osiris dead and went for help. But then Seth cut the body into pieces. He scattered them throughout Egypt. When Isis found the pieces, she used them to turn Osiris into the first mummy.

Osiris went to rule the underworld. Isis gave birth to their son Horus. People had suffered from lack of rain and food with Seth in charge. When Horus was grown, he fought his uncle for Egypt. Their struggle went on so long that the other gods set up a court to decide the winner.

Isis went to Seth's palace pretending to be a beautiful young woman. She told Seth her story without using names. Seth said that the man who killed her husband must be punished. When Isis revealed herself, the court found Seth guilty and threw him out of Egypt.

QUEST FOR THE GOLDEN FLEECE

The Greek hero Jason was the prince of Iolcus. When he was young, his uncle Pelias

EGYPTIAN GODS AND GODDESSES

God or Goddess	Roles in Myth	Often Appears As	Roles in Religion
Osiris	The slain king	A mummy with crossed arms holding farming tools	Ruler of the dead with the power to give life
Isis	Wife of the slain king	A beautiful woman with a sun and cow's horns on her head	A magical healer and divine mother
Seth	Murderer of Osiris	A character with a dog's body, ears with square tips, a tufted tail, and a curving, pointed nose	Sky god and god of war
Horus	Son of Osiris	A falcon or falcon-headed figure with one eye representing the sun and the other the moon	One of the greatest sky gods

Gods and goddesses often have unique appearances. Many of them have both human and animal traits.

seized the kingdom from the king. Jason fled before Pelias could harm him.

When Jason was grown, he returned to claim the throne. Pelias agreed to step

Medea played a large role in the myth about Jason. The sorceress helped the hero steal the Golden Fleece from her father.

aside. But he was only pretending. He ordered Jason to bring him the Golden Fleece. This wool was from a divine ram. It belonged to King Aeëtes (ee-EE-teez) of Colchis.

When Jason asked Aeëtes for the fleece, the king gave Jason three tasks. He had to plow a field with fiery bulls. He then had to sow the soil with dragon teeth. Finally, Jason had to defeat a human army that grew from the teeth.

Aeëtes's daughter Medea fell in love with Jason. She was a **sorceress**. She used her magic to help him.

The Roman poet Ovid wrote stories of Greek and Roman myths in the first century CE. He explained Jason's victory over the magical army. Ovid wrote, "He threw a boulder into the midst of his enemies and this turned their attack, on him, against themselves."[1]

Aeëtes still refused to give up the fleece. Medea helped Jason steal it. Aeëtes chased after them. Medea slowed Aeëtes down by killing her own brother. She knew their father would stop to bury his son. This gave Jason and Medea time to escape.

Back in Iolcus, Pelias refused to give Jason the throne. So Medea tricked the king's daughters into killing him. But then Jason and Medea had to flee. Jason never became king.

QUEST FOR HOME

Aeneas was a Trojan in Roman mythology. After the Greeks burned the city of Troy, Aeneas escaped. His wife died among the flames and fighting. Her ghost told him he had a great **destiny**. She said he would create a city in Italy and become an ancestor of all Romans. Aeneas set sail

MYTHICAL JOURNEYS

Much of Aeneas's travels in the *Aeneid* were modeled on the journey featured in an older **epic**, the *Odyssey*. The *Odyssey* told of the Greek hero Odysseus's return home after the Trojan War. The *Odyssey* also inspired events in the *Argonautica*. This was an epic telling of Jason's story.

with a band of followers. They landed at Carthage in North Africa.

Aeneas fell in love with Queen Dido of Carthage. But the gods warned Aeneas. They said he still hadn't reached the place that would become home for the Trojans. Aeneas and his people sailed on.

Furious and heartbroken, Dido cursed the Trojans. She then took her own life. The *Aeneid* is an epic poem by Virgil from the first century BCE. It tells the story of Aeneas's quest. In it, Dido vowed that Carthage would always be the enemy of Aeneas's people. She said, "Let no lover

Although Aeneas fell in love with Queen Dido, he knew he couldn't stay with her in Carthage. His destiny lay ahead of him in a different place.

or treaty unite the nations! Arise from my ashes, unknown avenger, to harass the Trojan settlers with fire and sword."[2]

Aeneas went on to land in Italy. King Latinus welcomed him, but other tribes attacked the Trojans. After a war, Aeneas made peace and founded his new city, Lavinium. He had achieved his destiny.

2
MONSTER SLAYERS

Heroes often have to slay one or more monsters. Sometimes a villain gives a hero that goal. A monster may be a threat to the world. Monsters terrify the characters in the story. They may also frighten the story's audience. A hero who fails may not survive.

SLAYER GOD

In Babylonian myth, the universe began with **chaos**. Out of the chaos came the god Apsu and the goddess Tiamat. The couple had many divine children.

Apsu hated his noisy children and wanted to kill them. Tiamat did not. But then

Tiamat (left) is often depicted as a dragon-like monster. Although Marduk (right) was said to have four heads, he often appears in art with just one.

her son Ea slayed Apsu. The killing made Tiamat angry. Her temper grew worse when Ea fathered Marduk. As a weather god, Marduk controlled the wind and waves. He had four heads with flashing eyes and tongues of fire.

Tiamat prepared for war. She married a demon and gave birth to an army of monsters. Marduk agreed to fight the monsters if the gods made him their king.

Tiamat became a dragon-like monster. Marduk attacked her with the wind. It filled Tiamat's mouth so she couldn't eat Marduk. He slayed her with an arrow.

Tiamat's death helped Marduk create the world. Half of her body became the sky while the other half became the earth.

Marduk made the heavens and the earth from Tiamat's body. The gods killed her demon husband. They created the first human from his body. Marduk took charge of all the other gods and the human world.

HERO TWINS

The Maya hero twins were Hunahpu (woo-nuh-POO) and Xbalanque (sh-bah-lahn-KAY). Their father and his brother once played a noisy ball game. This angered the Lords of Death. They challenged the brothers to a game in the realm of the dead. The brothers lost. The lords then killed the brothers.

Hunahpu and Xbalanque decided to avenge their father. They played ball loudly to get the lords' attention. The lords commanded the heroes to entertain them in the realm of the dead. The heroes played

A carving found in El Mirador in Guatemala depicts Hunahpu and Xbalanque. Scientists think this settlement was the center of Maya civilization.

a trick. Hunahpu and Xbalanque sacrificed each other. To sacrifice someone is to kill them as a divine offering. But the twins used their powers to bring each other back to life.

The lords grew excited. A text called the *Popol Vuh* was written in the 1500s.

Seven Macaw took great pride in his metal wings and teeth made of gems. But his pride angered the gods.

It tells the story of this myth. In it, the lords said, "Do it to us! Sacrifice us!"[3] The heroes obeyed. But they did not bring the lords back to life.

The twins' work was not done. A bird demon named Seven Macaw offended the gods. Precious metals formed his wings while brilliant gems formed his teeth. He claimed to be the sun and the moon. The other gods ordered the twins to deal with the demon.

The twins shot Seven Macaw with a blowgun, hurting his teeth. The heroes then asked two older gods to help with their plan. The older gods told Seven Macaw

THE *POPOL VUH*

When the *Popol Vuh* was written, the Spanish were banning Maya religions and burning Maya books. The authors of the *Popol Vuh* wanted to save the stories for their people. The writers' names are unknown. But experts think they were members of the K'iche (kee-CHAY) Maya nobility.

they could heal him. Instead, they removed all his precious metals and gems. Now plain, Seven Macaw melted away. As a reward for their success at monster-slaying, Hunahpu and Xbalanque became the sun and the moon.

DRAGON SLAYER

Sigurd was a Norse hero raised by a smith, or metalworker, named Regin. After Sigurd became an adult, Regin challenged the hero with a task. Regin wanted Sigurd to slay the dragon Fafnir. Fafnir guarded a great treasure of gold.

Regin asked Sigurd to slay a dragon named Fafnir. Regin wanted the treasure the fierce creature guarded.

Regin made Sigurd a strong sword for his attack. But Regin had an evil plan. He advised Sigurd to dig a hole and hide in it. Sigurd could stab Fafnir as the dragon passed overhead. The dragon's blood would fill the hole and drown Sigurd.

Sigurd did not realize the gold he took from Fafnir was cursed. The treasure would always lead its owner to death.

A story called the *Volsunga* **Saga** was written around 1270. It told what happened next. It said, "Sigurd fell to digging . . . a pit, and while he was at that work, there came to him an old man with a long beard."[4] The man was the god Odin in disguise. Odin warned Sigurd to dig several holes to drain the blood away from the hero.

Sigurd stabbed the dragon and avoided drowning. When Sigurd tasted some of the blood, he gained the ability to understand birds. The birds told Sigurd that Regin still planned to kill him. Sigurd killed Regin instead. The hero took the treasure for himself.

3

AT WAR

Many heroes and villains take part in mythical wars. Some lead their people into battle as rulers or great warriors. Some heroes stand alone against an entire army.

Huang Di was called the Yellow Emperor in Chinese mythology. This hero god made many inventions for his people. He designed boats, clothes, and mirrors. He also fought many wars.

Huang Di ruled the center of ancient China. He was a kind leader. Yan Di, who ruled to the south, was not. The two rulers began to fight. Huang Di had the support

Huang Di is still greatly respected in China. A marble statue of the emperor is displayed at a temple for him in Henan.

of many animals. Bears, wolves, and big cats fought in his armies. Some fights were brutal. Blood flowed from one battle like a stream. After a long war, Huang Di won.

Later, a monster named Chiyou attacked Huang Di. Chiyou had horns and armor on his head. Demons filled Chiyou's army.

Huang Di began by attacking the army with thirst. He told a dragon to take away the earth's water. Chiyou ordered weather gods to start a huge rainstorm. Huang Di ordered a goddess to dry up the world.

Chiyou could fly. Huang Di had to catch and kill him to end the war. First, Huang

Huang Di's drum was loud enough to be heard from many miles away. The thundering sound kept Chiyou on the ground where the hero could kill the monster.

Di killed a one-legged monster who could create storms. The emperor made a drum from the monster's skin. The great noise from the drum thundered through the sky. The sound overcame Chiyou. He was unable to lift off the ground. This made it possible for Huang Di to finally slay his enemy.

Huang Di went on to live for 300 years. Some myths say he became immortal. He was an ancestor of many other heroes.

CUCHULAINN

The hero Cuchulainn (KOO-kul-in) was the son of the Celtic god Lugh. Cuchulainn had a total of fourteen fingers, fourteen toes, and fourteen **pupils** in his eyes. He looked even more monstrous when he flew into a rage. History professor Mark Cartwright wrote, "During this fury, his body is warped with parts shifting about, his crown spurts columns of blood and a great light."[5]

Cuchulainn was sent to study with the warrior woman Scáthach (SKAH-hahk) in Scotland. There, he made a great friend named Ferdiad. Scáthach gave Cuchulainn a spear that created thirty wounds at once.

HOUND OF CULANN

Cuchulainn means "hound of Culann" in Old Irish. The hero received this name as a child after killing the guard dog of a man named Culann. Although he killed the animal in self-defense, Cuchulainn wanted to make up for it. He served as Culann's guard dog until he found the man another animal.

Cuchulainn and Ferdiad became great friends. But their bond could not stop one of them from killing the other.

Cuchulainn took part in a famous war. It protected the territory of Ulster from the armies of Connacht. Ulster and Connacht were both regions of Ireland. Queen Medb of Connacht wanted to steal a valuable bull from Ulster to increase her wealth.

Ulster had a weakness. The goddess Macha had cursed the region. If attacked, all the men of Ulster fell down in terrible pain for several days. When Queen Medb attacked, only Cuchulainn avoided the curse. The hero was able to do this because he hadn't been born in Ulster. He stood against the attack, taking on warriors one by one. He killed them all.

Ferdiad was on Queen Medb's side. She forced him to face Cuchulainn. Neither warrior wanted to kill the other. The two friends battled for several days. Every night they sent each other gifts. Finally, Cuchulainn was forced to slay his old friend with his magic spear. When the Ulster warriors recovered, they defeated Queen Medb's armies. But it was too late to save Ferdiad.

WARRIOR WOMEN

Two female warriors from Norse myth carried the name Hervor. The first Hervor's father had been buried with a magic sword called Tyrfing. The weapon would always bring victory. When her father died, Hervor summoned his ghost. She asked for the sword. He opened his grave and gave her Tyrfing.

Hervor disguised herself as a man for battle. She went by the name Hervard when fighting. A saga from the 1200s tells how she used her skills. The writing was called *The Saga of Hervor and Heidrek*. It said,

A VIKING WARRIOR WOMAN

In 1878, people discovered a grave in Sweden. It dated to the 900s, the time of the Vikings. Weapons filled the tomb. The clothing on the body suggested the person had been an important warrior. In 2017, scientists tested the remains. They identified the person as a woman.

Norse mythology had two brave heroines named Hervor. They were connected by blood and also through the magic sword they both used to fight in battle.

"Hervor spent a long time in warfare and raiding, and had great success."[6] Afterward, she went home. She returned to doing the things other women did, such as weaving and embroidering.

Hervor's granddaughter was also named Hervor. The granddaughter received the sword after her father's death. Later, an army marched on Hervor's brother, King Angantyr. Hervor quickly gathered the few warriors she could find to face her brother's enemy.

Hervor led her troops into battle. She died fighting alongside them. Hearing of her bravery, Angantyr's warriors who hadn't taken part in the fight took courage. In the end, Angantyr won the war.

4
MYTHICAL LEADERS

Some mythical leaders become heroes through great deeds. Others are villains who do evil things. Some leaders ride into battle at the head of their followers. They may gain victory or fall in ruin.

WOLF KING

Lycaon was a wicked king in Greek mythology. His people were also evil. Some even murdered their own kin out of greed. Things got so bad on Earth that the god Zeus decided to go there himself.

Lycaon tried to trick Zeus. But the powerful Greek god struck the king's palace with lightning. He then turned the wicked leader into a wolf.

Many cultures have myths about a god wiping out all humans. Humanity is then restarted, usually with one man and one woman.

Zeus visited Lycaon's palace. When Zeus announced that he was divine, almost everyone began to worship him. But Lycaon mocked the others for believing Zeus.

Next, the king arranged a cruel surprise for dinner. After killing his own son, Lycaon served his flesh to Zeus. But Zeus couldn't be fooled. He destroyed the palace with lightning. The Roman poet Ovid wrote, "[Lycaon] himself ran in terror, and reaching the silent fields howled aloud, frustrated of speech."[7] Zeus had punished him by turning him into a wolf.

Zeus's anger didn't stop there. He killed nearly all humans with a flood. Only one man and one woman survived. Together they restarted humanity.

A LEADING WOMAN

In Czech mythology, the woman Vlasta led a tribe of other warrior women. Vlasta trained the women, turning them into a fierce army. They built the mighty Devin Castle upon a great hill.

When Prince Premsyl's army attacked the castle, the men expected an easy victory. But the female warriors attacked the men with a rush of arrows, horses, and warriors. Vlasta and her army killed every warrior they faced that day.

The tide of the war turned when the women killed the bravest male warrior, Ctirad (TSKIH-rat). The women set a trap. They tied one of their own warriors to a tree. When Ctirad stopped to help her,

The female warriors attacked the male army with great skill. In addition to physical weapons, they also used strategy against their enemies.

the other women killed him. They then displayed Ctirad's body at Devin Castle. When the remaining male warriors saw this, they stormed the castle. Vlasta made a mistake. She let the men surround her. The men killed her and all her warriors.

Devin Castle is a real structure that still stands today. Its ancient name was Dowina, which comes from a Slavic word meaning "girl."

This left Premsyl as the sole ruler of the Czech tribes.

TAMING THE FLOOD

The Chinese hero Yu had the task of taming a great flood. Some myths depict Yu as a dragon. Others show him as a god who looked like a man. Yu's mother ate a magic pearl or seed to get pregnant. In other versions, Yu came out of the body of his father Gun.

The supreme god told Yu to control the flood using magical soil. Yu built dams. He also lowered the water level. He had a dragon who used its tail to make channels in the earth. They moved water out to sea.

Yu also dealt with monsters. One was the spirit of the wild Huai River. The spirit looked like a monkey. Its neck could stretch as high as a tall tree. Yu asked a god to chain up the spirit. With the spirit captured, Yu could control the river.

Yu worked for many years to tame the great flood. He succeeded in this task. As a reward, the current king chose Yu as China's next emperor.

Stories of heroes and villains are found in mythologies around the world. People continue to tell these stories in books and

MORTAL HEROES

Many myths focus on the gods. But hero myths can center on a human character. Heroes are among the first humans in ancient writings. They may have great powers, but they suffer and die like other mortals. Only their great deeds live on.

Yu was rewarded well for his efforts in stopping the great flood. According to the myth, he became the next emperor of China.

movies. The myth of the hero isn't just important in its ancient form. People also tell stories of new heroes and villains. Some are made up while others are real. Either way, these stories continue to inspire people.

GLOSSARY

chaos

disorder and confusion

destiny

an established course of events that are meant to happen to someone in the future

divine

having to do with gods or goddesses

epic

a long story or poem telling the deeds of heroes

pupils

circular black areas in the center of eyes

saga

a long story about heroes and adventure

sorceress

a female magic user

version

a form of something that is different from other forms

SOURCE NOTES

CHAPTER ONE: ON A QUEST

1. A.S. Kline, trans., "Book VII," *Metamorphoses*, n.d. http://ovid.lib.virginia.edu.

2. H.R. Fairclough, trans., "Aeneid Book 4," *Theoi Project*, n.d. www.theoi.com.

CHAPTER TWO: MONSTER SLAYERS

3. Dennis Tedlock, trans., "Popol Vuh: The Mayan Book of the Dawn of Life," *Google Books*, n.d. https://books.google.com.

4. William Morris and Eirikr Magnusson, trans., "Chapter 18," *Volsunga Saga, Tufts University*, 1888. www.perseus.tufts.edu.

CHATER THREE: AT WAR

5. Mark Cartwright, "Cú Chulainn," *World History Encyclopedia*, February 3, 2021. www.worldhistory.org.

6. Santa Jansone, "Ladies with Axes and Spears," *JSTOR*, 2014. www.jstor.org.

CHAPTER FOUR: MYTHICAL LEADERS

7. A.S. Kline, trans., "Book I," *Metamorphoses*, n.d. http://ovid.lib.virginia.edu.

FOR FURTHER RESEARCH

BOOKS

Amie Jane Leavitt, *Isis: Queen of the Egyptian Gods*. North Mankato, MN: Capstone Press, 2019.

Don Nardo, *Chinese Mythology*. San Diego, CA: BrightPoint Press, 2020.

Mathias Nordvig, *Norse Mythology for Kids: Tales of Gods, Creatures, and Quests*. Emeryville, CA: Rockridge Press, 2021.

INTERNET SOURCES

"Ancient Egypt," *DK Find Out!*, 2022. www.dkfindout.com.

"A Flood of Myths and Stories," *PBS*, February 14, 2020. www.pbs.org.

"Who Were the Ancient Greek Gods and Heroes?" *BBC Bitesize*, 2022. www.bbc.co.uk.

WEBSITES

In Search of Myths and Heroes
www.pbs.org/mythsandheroes

"In Search of Myths and Heroes" explores and compares different myths of heroes across cultures.

Living Maya Time: Sun, Corn, and the Calendar
http://maya.nmai.si.edu

"Living Maya Time" explores Maya culture, including the *Popol Vuh* and its myths.

Primary History KS2: Ancient Greece
www.bbc.co.uk

This site from the BBC has links to audio clips and transcripts telling several Greek myths, including ones about heroes.

INDEX

Aeneas, 21–22, 23
Argonautica, 21

Chiyou, 38, 39–40
Ctirad, 52–53
Cuchulainn, 40–41, 42, 43–44

Dido, 22–23

gods, 13–17, 25–27, 30, 35, 49–51

Hervor, 44–47
Horus, 15–16, 17
Huang Di, 36–40
Hunahpu, 28–30, 31–32

Isis, 13–14, 15, 16, 17

Jason, 16–17, 18, 19–20

leaders, 48, 49, 50–52, 54, 56
Lycaon, 49, 50, 51

Marduk, 26–27
Medb, 42–43, 44
Medea, 19, 20
monster slayers, 24, 26–27, 28–35
mortal heroes, 56

Odyssey, 21
Osiris, 13–15, 16, 17

Popol Vuh, 29–30, 31

quests, 12–13, 15, 18–20, 21–23

Regin, 32, 33, 35

Seth, 14–16, 17
Sigurd, 32, 33, 35

Vlasta, 51–52, 53

war, 36–40, 42–44, 45–46, 47

Yan Di, 37
Yi, 9
Yu, 54–56

Xbalanque, 28–30, 31–32

Zeus, 49–51

IMAGE CREDITS

Cover: © Delcarmat/Shutterstock Images
5: © Rudall 30/Shutterstock Images
7: © Paul Orr/Shutterstock Images
8: © Jian Ye Liu/Shutterstock Images
11: © Maxim Maksutov/Shutterstock Images
13: © Stanley Kalvan/Shutterstock Images
14: © Jakkarin Apikornrat/Shutterstock Images
17: © Red Line Editorial
18: © Meunierd/Shutterstock Images
23: © Prisma Archivo/Alamy
25: © Ivy Close Images/Alamy
27: © Andrew Mayovskyy/Shutterstock Images
29: © Anne Lewis/Alamy
30: © Vvoronov/Shutterstock Images
33: © Fer Gregory/iStockphoto
34: © Interfoto/History/Alamy
37: © F. Jack Jackson/Alamy
39: © NAK Photographer/Shutterstock Images
42: © Ardee Snapper/Alamy
46: © Gorev Evgenii/Shutterstock Images
49: © Delcarmat/Shutterstock Images
50: © Rat Pack 223/iStockphoto
53: © Stanislav Hubkin/iStockphoto
54: © TT Studio/Shutterstock Images
57: © Pictures From History/CPA Media Pte Ltd/Alamy

ABOUT THE AUTHOR

Clara MacCarald is a freelance writer who has written more than forty nonfiction books for kids. She lives with her daughter and a small herd of cats in an off-grid house nestled in the forests of central New York.